W9-AVC-415

SHARKS

TIGER SHARKS

JOHN F. PREVOST

ABDO & Daughters

J
597.31
Pre

Published by Abdo & Daughters, 4940 Viking Drive, Suite 622, Edina, Minnesota 55435.

Library bound edition distributed by Rockbottom Books, Pentagon Tower, P.O. Box 36036, Minneapolis, Minnesota 55435.

Printed in the United States.

Cover Photo credit: Peter Arnold, Inc.
Interior Photo credits: Peter Arnold, Inc. pages 7, 9, 11, 15, 17, 19, 21
Natural Selection, pages 5, 13

Edited by Bob Italia

Library of Congress Cataloging-in-Publication Data

Prevost, John F.
  Tiger Sharks / John F. Prevost.
    p. cm. — (Sharks)
Includes bibliographical references (p.23) and index.
  ISBN 1-56239-468-1
1. Tiger shark—Juvenile literature. [1. Tiger shark. 2. Sharks.]
I. Title. II. Series: Prevost, John F. Sharks.
QL638.95.C3P74 1995
597'.31—dc20
                                   95-2749
                                        CIP
                                        AC

ABOUT THE AUTHOR

John Prevost is a marine biologist and diver who has been active in conservation and education issues for the past 18 years. Currently he is living inland and remains actively involved in freshwater and marine husbandry, conservation and education projects.

Contents

TIGER SHARKS AND FAMILY

Sharks are fish without **scales**. A rough covering of tiny tooth-shaped **denticles** protects their skin. Sharks don't have bones. Their skeleton is made of **cartilage**, a tough, stretchy tissue. It is like the substance that makes up the human ear.

Tiger sharks are found in **temperate** and **tropical** ocean waters. Often they swim slowly. But they can swim fast when feeding or fleeing.

Tiger sharks are one of the most dangerous sharks to man. They are willing to try any type of food—including people! The smooth dogfish and requiem sharks are related to the tiger shark.

A tiger shark swimming near the ocean bottom.

WHAT THEY LOOK LIKE

Large female tiger sharks can be over 24 feet (7.4 meters) long. Most are less than 16.5 feet (5 meters) long. Male tiger sharks average 12 feet (3.7 meters).

Tiger sharks have big heads with large eyes and mouths. The tiger shark is named for its dark, tiger-stripe markings. These fade as the shark gets older.

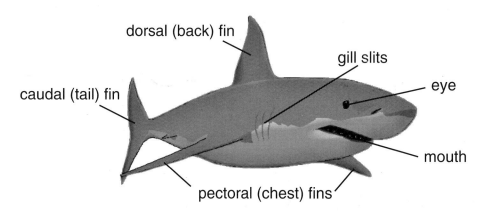

dorsal (back) fin

gill slits

eye

caudal (tail) fin

mouth

pectoral (chest) fins

Most sharks share the same features.

The tiger shark is named for its dark, tiger-stripe markings.

Tiger sharks are often found alone, but will form loose **schools** when feeding in areas with large numbers of **prey**. They like to feed at night.

WHERE THEY LIVE

Tiger sharks are found at night in **temperate** and **tropical** ocean waters, **bays**, **lagoons**, on **coral reefs**, river **estuaries**, inshore, or offshore. A tiger shark may form a territory that includes small ocean islands. Some sharks will **migrate** with the season to follow **prey**.

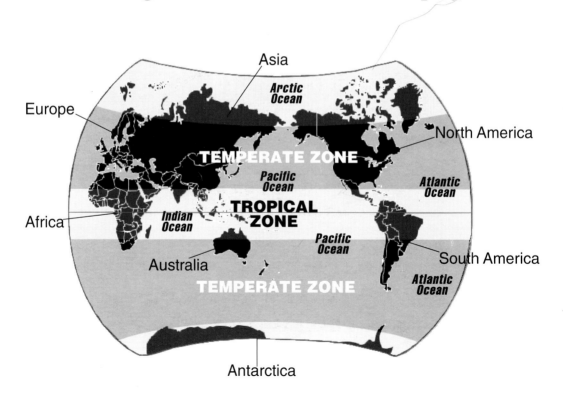

A scientist tags a tiger shark to follow its migration path.

Two different tiger shark **species** have been reported. Most experts believe there is only one species.

FOOD

All sharks are **predators**. They eat other animals. Tiger sharks will eat nearly anything in the water. Their **prey** includes bony fish, other sharks, **stingrays**, sea snakes, seals, dolphins, and sea birds. Armored prey such as **conchs**, lobsters, and sea turtles are also eaten. In shallow water and rivers, the tiger shark will feed on land birds and **mammals**.

Tiger sharks are well-known for the junk that is sometimes found in their bellies: pieces of coal and wood, seeds, feathers, plastic bags, cans, and small barrels. None of this junk is good for the shark. It just eats anything it can swallow.

Tiger sharks will eat nearly anything in the water.

SENSES

The tiger shark's large eyes allow it to see in dim water. A tiger shark has a good sense of smell. It can locate injured **prey** or dead animals from long distances.

Sharks can sense **electric fields** from prey. All animals with nervous systems give off a weak electric field. The shark's skill to sense this electric field helps it find hidden prey.

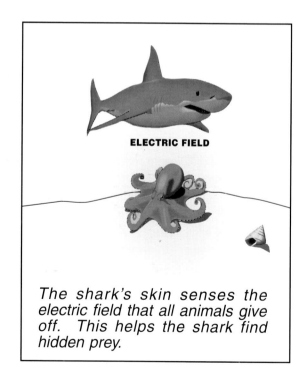

ELECTRIC FIELD

The shark's skin senses the electric field that all animals give off. This helps the shark find hidden prey.

The tiger shark's eyes are large and allow it to see in dim water.

BABIES

Tiger sharks are a common **species**. They have large **litters**, from 10 to 82 pups! The young hatch from eggs and are fed by a yolk sac inside their mother. Then they are born alive.

Birth happens in the spring and early summer in protected shallow areas. The young tiger sharks are small at birth, 20 to 30 inches (51 to 76 cm) long. Once they are born, the pups are on their own. Their mother does not raise them.

A diver watches a baby tiger shark off the Bahama Islands.

ATTACK AND DEFENSE

A tiger shark has a large mouth with 18 to 26 teeth per row. The tiger shark will eat whatever it can grab. So its teeth are made to cut or snag **prey**. These teeth are sharp and can cut its food.

A large tiger shark has little to fear except man or a larger shark. If frightened, the tiger shark can escape at great speed. The shark's hunting senses will also warn it of danger.

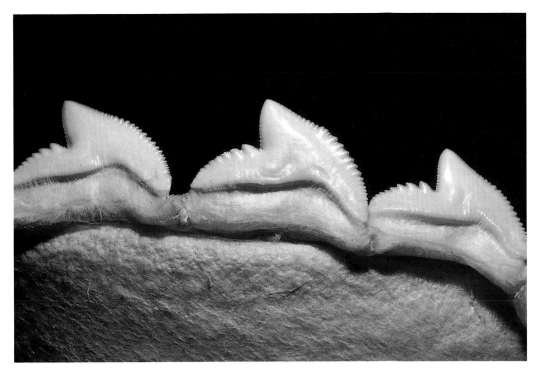

Tiger shark teeth in the lower jaw. These teeth are made to cut and snag prey.

ATTACKS ON HUMANS

The tiger shark is one of the most dangerous sharks to man. Only the great white shark has more reported attacks on divers, swimmers, and boats. But because they are big, great whites are sometimes blamed for tiger shark attacks.

There are more tiger sharks than great white sharks. The tiger shark is curious and is not afraid of divers. But the number of attacks on humans is low. Only 25 to 30 deaths from tiger shark attacks are reported yearly all over the world. Fishermen kill millions of sharks each year.

The tiger shark is curious and not afraid of divers. This diver is a researcher who is about to release this tiger shark.

TIGER SHARK FACTS

Scientific Name:

Tiger Shark   *Galeocerdo curvier*

Possible second species: *G. rayneri*

Average Size: 12 feet (3.7 meters) - males

16.5 feet (5 meters) - females

24 feet (7.4 meters) - largest female

Where They're Found: All over the world in **temperate** and **tropical** seas.

The tiger shark.

GLOSSARY

Bay: An arm of a sea or lake extending into the land.

Cartilage (KAR-till-ij): A tough and stretchy type of tissue, like gristle.

Conch (kongk): A saltwater animal having a large spiral shell.

Coral: A hard substance resembling limestone, usually found in tropical waters.

Denticle (DEN-tih-kull): A small tooth-like structure that protects a shark's skin and makes it rough to the touch.

Electric field: An electric-charged area surrounding an animal's body, created by the nervous system.

Estuary (ES-tew-air-ee): The mouth of a river where the current meets the sea.

Gill slits: A part of the body of a fish by which it gets oxygen from water.

Lagoon: A shallow body of water partly cut off from the sea by a narrow strip of land.

Litter: Young animals born at one time.

Mammals: Warm-blooded animals with backbones that feed their young milk.

Migrate: To move seasonally from one climate or region to another.

Pelvic fin: A fin found at the lower part of a fish's body.

Predator (PRED-a-tor): An animal that hunts and eats other animals.

Prey: An animal that is hunted for food.

Reef: A narrow ridge of coral at or near the water surface.
Scales: Platelike structures forming all or part of the outer covering of certain animals, such as snakes and fish.
Schools: A large group of fish or water animals of the same kind swimming together.
Stingray: A large fish having a flat body and a whiplike tail with a poisonous spine.
Species (SPEE-seas): A group of related living things that shares basic characteristics.
Temperate (TEM-prit): Moderate to cool water located between the cold polar waters and the warmer tropical waters.
Tropical (TRAH-pih-kull): A region of the Earth lying between the Tropic of Cancer and the Tropic of Capricorn.

BIBLIOGRAPHY

Budker, Paul. *The Life of Sharks*. London: Weidenfeld and Nicolson,1971.

Compagno, Leonard. FAO Species Catalogue Vol. 4, *Sharks of the World*. United Nations Development Programme, Rome, 1984.

Gilbert, P. W., ed. *Sharks, Skates, and Rays*. Maryland: Johns Hopkins Press, 1967.

Macquitty, Miranda. *Shark*. New York: Alfred A. Knopf, 1992.

Sattler, Helen. *Shark, the Super Fish*. New York: Lothrop, Lee & Shepard Books, 1986.

Server, Lee. *Sharks*. New York City: Gallery Books, 1990.

Index